US $9.99

£7.99

Classic Cocktails

The most popular classics
Blend, build, shake and stir!

NEW
HOLLAND

INTRODUCTION

METHODS OF MIXING COCKTAILS

The four methods below are the most common processes of mixing cocktails:

Shake

Stir

Build

Blend

Shake

To shake is to mix a cocktail by shaking it in a cocktail shaker by hand. First, fill the glass part of the shaker three quarters full with ice, then pour the ingredients on top of the ice. Less expensive ingredients are usually poured before the deluxe ingredients, just in case you make a mistake! Pour the contents of the glass into the metal part of the shaker and shake vigorously for ten to fifteen seconds.

Remove the glass section and using a Hawthorn strainer, strain contents into the cocktail glass. Shaking ingredients that do not mix easily with spirits is easy and practical (eg juices, egg whites, cream and sugar syrups).

Most shakers have two or three parts. In a busy bar, the cap is often temporarily misplaced. If this happens, a coaster or the inside palm of your hand is quite effective.

American shakers are best.

To sample the cocktail before serving to the customer, pour a small amount into the shaker cap and using a straw check the taste.

Stir

To stir a cocktail is to mix the ingredients by stirring them with ice in a mixing glass and then straining them into a chilled cocktail glass. Short circular twirls are most preferred. (NB. The glass part of a shaker will do well for this.) Spirits, liqueurs and vermouths that blend easily together are mixed by this method.

Build

To build a cocktail is to mix the ingredients in the glass in which the cocktail is to be served, floating

one on top of the other. Hi-ball, long fruit juice and carbonated mixed cocktails are typically built using this technique. Where possible a swizzle stick should be put into the drink to mix the ingredients after being presented to the customer.
Long straws are excellent substitutes when swizzle sticks are unavailable.

Blend

To blend a cocktail is to mix the ingredients using an electric blender/ mixer. It is recommended to add the fruit (fresh or tinned) first. Slicing small pieces gives a smoother texture than if you add the whole fruit.

Next, pour the alcohol. Ice should always be added last. This order ensures that the fruit is blended freely with the alcoholic ingredients and allows the ice to gradually mix into the beverage, chilling it. Ideally,

the blender should be on for at least 20 seconds.

Following this procedure will prevent ice and fruit lumps that then need to be strained.

If the blender starts to rattle and hum, ice may be obstructing the blades from spinning. Always check that the blender is clean before you start. Angostura Bitters is alcohol based which is suitable for cleaning. Fill 4 to 5 shakes with hot water, rinse and then wipe clean.

TECHNIQUES IN MAKING COCKTAILS

Shake and Pour

After shaking the cocktail, pour the contents straight into the glass. When pouring into highball glasses and some old-fashioned glasses the ice Cubes are included. This eliminates straining.

Share and Strain

Using a Hawthorn strainer (or knife) this technique prevents the ice going into the glass.
Straining protects the cocktail ensuring melted ice won't dilute the mixture.

Float Ingredients

Hold the spoon right way up and rest

it with the lip slightly above the level of the last layer. Fill spoon gently and the contents will flow smoothly from all around the rim. Use the back of the spoon's dish only if you are experienced.

Frosting (sugar and salt rims)

This technique is used to coat the rim of the glass with either salt or sugar. First, rub lemon/orange slice juice all the way around the glassrim.

Next, holding the glass upside down by the stem, rest on a plate containing salt or sugar and turn slightly so that it adheres to the glass.

Pressing the glass too deeply into the salt or sugar often results in chunks sticking to the glass.

A lemon slice is used for salt and an orange slice is used for sugar.

To achieve colour affects, put a small amount of grenadine or coloured liqueur in a plate and coat the rim of the glass, then gently place in the sugar. The sugar absorbs the grenadine, which turns it pink.

This is much easier than mixing grenadine with sugar and then trying to get it to stick to the glass.

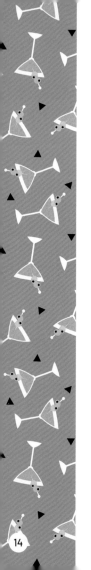

DESCRIPTION OF LIQUEURS & SPIRITS

Advocaat: A combination of fresh egg whites, yolks, sugar, brandy, vanilla and spirit. Limited shelf life. Recommended shelf life 12–15 months from date of manufacture.

Amaretto: A rich subtle liqueur with a unique almond taste.

Angostura Bitters: An essential part of any bar or kitchen. A unique additive whose origins date back to 1824. A mysterious blend of natural herbs and spices, it is a seasoning agent in both sweet and savoury dishes and drinks. Ideal for dieters as it is low in sodium and calories.

Bailey's Irish Cream: The largest selling liqueur in the world. It is a blend of Irish whisky, softened by Irish cream. It is a natural product.

Banana Liqueur: Fresh ripe bananas are the perfect base for the definitive daiquiri and a host of other exciting fruit cocktails.

Benedictine: A perfect end to a perfect meal. Serve straight, with ice, soda, or as part of a favourite cocktail.

Bourbon: Has a smooth, deep, easy taste.

Brandy: Smooth and mild spirit, is considered very smooth and palatable, ideal for mixing.

Campari: A drink for many occasions, both as a long or short drink, or as a key ingredient in many fashionable cocktails.

Cassis: Deep, rich purple promises and delivers a regal and robust taste and aroma. Cassis lends itself to neat drinking or an endless array of delicious sauces and desserts.

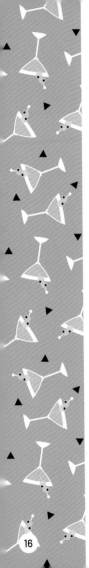

Chartreuse: A liqueur available in either yellow or green colour. Made by the monks of the Carthusian order. The only world famous liqueur still made by monks.

Cherry Advocaat: Same as Advocaat, infused with natural cherry.

Cherry Brandy: Is made from concentrated, morello cherry juice. Small quantity of bitter almonds and vanilla is added to make it more enjoyable as a neat drink before or after dinner. Excellent for mixers, topping, ice cream, fruit salads, pancakes, etc.

Coconut Liqueur: A smooth liqueur, composed of exotic coconut, heightened with light-bodied white rum.

Cointreau: Made from a neutral grain spirit, as opposed to cognac. An aromatic taste of natural citrus fruits.

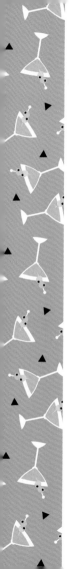

A great mixer or over ice. Crème de cacao – dark: Rich, deep chocolate. Smooth and classy. Serve on its own, or mix for all kinds of delectable treats.

Crème de cacao – white: This liqueur delivers a powerfully lively, full bodied chocolate taste. Excellent ingredient when absence of colour is desired.

Crème de menthe – green: Clear peppermint flavour, reminiscent of a fresh, crisp, clean winter's day in the mountains. Excellent mixer, a necessity in the gourmet kitchen.

Crème de menthe – white: As Crème de menthe – green, when colour is not desired.

Curaçao – blue: Same as Triple Sec, brilliant blue colour is added to make some cocktails more exciting.

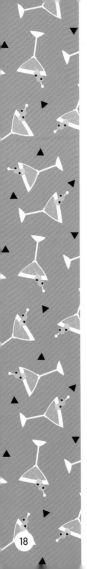

Curaçao – orange: Again, same as above, but stronger in orange, colouring is used for other varieties of cocktail mixers.

Curaçao Triple Sec: Based on natural citrus fruits. Well known fact is citrus fruits are the most important aromatic taste constituents. As a liqueur one of the most versatile. Can be enjoyed with or without ice as a neat drink, or used in mixed cocktails more than any other liqueur. Triple Sec – also known as white curaçao.

Galliano – vanilla: The distinguished taste! A classic liqueur that blends with a vast array of mixed drinks.

Gin: Its aroma comes from using the highest quality juniper berries and other rare and subtle herbs. Perfect mixer for both short and long drinks.

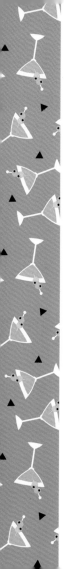

Kirsch: A fruit brandy distilled from morello cherries. Delicious drunk straight and excellent in a variety of food recipes.

Drambuie: A Scotch whisky liqueur. Made from a secret recipe dating back to 1745. "Dram Buidheach" the drink that satisfies.

Frangelico: A precious liqueur imported from Italy. Made from wild hazelnuts with infusions of berries and flowers to enrich the taste.

Grand Marnier: An original blend of fine old cognac and an extract of oranges. The recipe is over 150 years old.

Kahlúa: A smooth, dark liqueur made from real coffee and fine clear spirits. Its origins are based in Mexico.

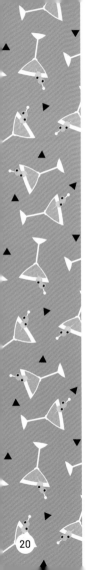

Malibu: A clear liqueur based on white rum with the subtle addition of coconut. Its distinctive taste blends naturally with virtually every mixer available.

Melon Liqueur: Soft green, exudes freshness. Refreshing and mouth-watering honeydew melon. Simple yet complex. Smooth on the palate, serve on the rocks, or use to create summertime cocktails.

Ouzo: The traditional spirit aperitif of Greece. The distinctive taste is derived mainly from the seed of the anise plant. A neutral grain spirit.

Peach Schnapps: Crystal clear, light liqueur, bursting with the taste of ripe peaches. Drink chilled, on the rocks or mix with any soft drink or juice.

Rum: A smooth, dry, light bodied rum, especially suited for drinks in which you require subtle aroma.

Rye Whiskey: Distilled from corn, rye and malted barley. A light, mild and delicate whiskey, ideal for drinking straight or in mixed cocktails.

Sambuca – clear: The Italian electric taste experience. Made from elder berries with a touch of anise.

Sambuca – black: An exciting encounter between Sambuca di Galliano & extracts of black elderberry.

Scotch Whisky: A whisky made in Scotland based on malt or grain. Similar taste to bourbon but with an added bite.

Southern Comfort: A liqueur not a bourbon as often thought. It is a unique, full-bodied liqueur with a touch of sweetness. Its recipe is a secret, but it is known to be based on peaches and apricots.

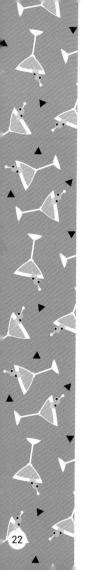

Strawberry Liqueur: Fluorescent red, unmistakable strawberry bouquet. Natural liqueur delivers a true to nature, fresh strawberry taste.

Tennessee Whiskey: Contrary to popular belief, this is not a bourbon, it is a distinctive product called Tennessee Whiskey. Made from the 'old sour mash' process. Leached through hard maple charcoal, then aged in charred white oak barrels, at a controlled temperature, acquiring body, bouquet and colour, yet remaining smooth.

Tequila: Distilled from the Mexcal variety of the cacti plant. A perfect mixer or drink straight with salt and lemon.

Tia Maria: A liqueur with a cane spirit base, and its taste derived from the finest Jamaican coffee. It is not too sweet with a subtle taste of coffee.

Vermouth: By description, vermouth is a herbally infused wine.

Three styles are most prevalent, these are:

Rosso: A bitter sweet herbal taste, often drunk as an aperitif.

Bianco: Is light, fruity and refreshing. Mixes well with soda, lemonade and fruit juices.

Dry: Is crisp, light and dry and is used as a base for many cocktails.

Vodka: The second largest selling spirit in the world. Most vodkas are steeped in tanks containing charcoal, removing all odours and impurities, making a superior quality product

The
Classics

PIÑA COLADA

Glass: Hurricane or tall glass
Garnish: Maraschino cherry or a slice of fresh pineapple

60 ml (2 oz) light rum
60 ml (2 oz) pineapple juice
60 ml (2 oz) coconut cream (chilled)

- Pour rum, juice and coconut cream into a blender over a large amount of crushed ice.

- Blend until slushy and pour into a chilled hurricane glass.

- If desitred garnish with a maraschino cherry or a slice of pineapple then serve with a straw.

- This drink may also be prepared in a cocktail shaker over a large amount of crushed ice if preferred.

FROZEN DAIQUIRI

Glass: Coupe
Garnish: Lemon wedges

60 ml (2 fl oz) Bacardi
45 ml (1 ½ fl oz) lime juice
30 ml (1 fl oz) sugar syrup

- Pour ingredients over a two handfuls of crushed ice and blend until smooth then pour into chilled glass.

Sometimes the taste of this drink can be diluted by blending it over ice. For a more intense drink, try using either a dark rum or a dark sugar syrup.

Variations:

Mango Daiquiri: replace half the rum with 15 ml (1/2 fl oz) Cointreau and 15 ml (1/2 fl oz) mango liqueur, and add half a diced fresh mango before blending.

Banana Daiquiri: replace a quarter of the rum with 15 ml (1/2 fl oz) banana liqueur, and add half a diced banana before blending.

FROZEN MARGARITA

Glass: Margarita
Garnish: Lime wheel

60 ml (2 fl oz) tequila
30 ml (1 fl oz) lime juice
15 ml (½ fl oz) Cointreau

- Add ingredients to blender over crushed ice and blend until smooth.

MARGARITA

Glass: Margarita
Garnish: Lime wheel on edge of glass and salt rim

60 ml (2 fl oz) tequila
30 ml (1 fl oz) lime juice
30 ml (1 fl oz) Cointreau

- Pour ingredients into a cocktail shaker over ice and shake.

- Strain into chilled glass.

ESPRESSO MARTINI

Glass: Martini
Garnish: 3 coffee beans

30 ml freshly brewed espresso coffee
30 ml vodka
30 ml Kahlua
5 ml sugar syrup (optional)

- Pour ingredients into a cocktail shaker over ice and shake vigorously. Double strain into chilled glass.

- Mixture must be shaken hard and strained/poured immediately to create the crema that sits on top of the cocktail.

Variations:
Frangelico: Replace Kahlua with 30 ml Frangelico.
Vanilla: Either replace vodka with vanilla vodka, or use the following proportions: 30 ml fresh espresso, 20 ml vodka, 20 ml Kahlua, 20 ml vanilla Galliano. Salted caramel: Replace half the Kahlua with 15 ml vanilla Galliano. Replace sugar syrup with 15 ml salted caramel syrup.
Rum: Replace vodka with spiced rum.
Irish: Replace vodka with Jamesons.

MAI TAI

Glass: Highball
Garnish: Pineapple spear, orange slice, mint leaves, tropical flowers if desired and limes all optional.

Serve with straws.

30 ml (1 fl oz) rum
15 ml (½ fl oz) dark rum
30 ml (1 fl oz) orange curacao
15 ml (½ fl oz) Amaretto
30 ml (1 fl oz) sugar syrup
30 ml (1 fl oz) lemon juice
15-30 ml sugar syrup
½ fresh lime, juiced

- Pour ingredients into a cocktail shaker over ice and shake. Strain over fresh ice.

Grenadine is often added to redden a glowing effect while the rum may be floated on top when served without straws.

RAFFLES SINGAPORE SLING

Glass: Hurricane or highball
Garnish: A slice of pineaplle and cherry

30ml (1 fl oz) Gin
30ml (1 fl oz) Cherry Brandy
15ml (½ fl oz) Bénédictine
15ml (½ fl oz) Cointreau
Dash Angostura Bitters
30ml (1 fl oz) Fresh Lime Juice
30ml (1 fl oz) Fresh Orange Juice
30ml (1 fl oz) Pineapple Juice
Slice of Orange
Sprig of Fresh Mint

- Pour Gin, Brandy, Bénédictine, Cointreau, Bitters and juices into a cocktail shaker over ice.

- Shake and strain into a highball glass over ice.

DRY MARTINI

Glass: Martini
Garnish: Green olives

60 ml (2 oz) dry gin
10-15 ml (⅓-½ oz) dry vermouth

- Pour gin and vermouth into a mixing glass over ice then stir until liquid is chilled.

- Strain into a chilled martini glass, add olives then serve.

DIRTY MARTINI

Glass: Martini
Garnish: Green olives

60 ml (2 oz) dry gin
10-15 ml (⅓-½ oz) dry vermouth
Add 15 ml (½ fl oz) olive brine

- Pour gin and vermouth into a mixing glass over ice and then add olivebrine then stir until liquid is chilled.

- Strain into a chilled martini glass, add olives then serve.

BLOODY MARY

Glass: Highball
Garnish: Celery stalk, lemon slice

60 ml (2 fl oz) vodka
120 ml (4 fl oz) tomato juice
salt and pepper to taste
Worcestershire sauce to taste
celery salt, optional
Tabasco sauce to taste
lemon juice to taste

- Pour ingredients into a mixing glass over ice and stir. Strain into glass and serve.

- Remember to add the spices first, then vodka and lemon juice followed by tomato juice. The celery stick is not just part of the garnish, so feel free to nibble as you drink.

The glass may also be salt-rimmed.

Feel free to play around with the garnish, suggestions include cucumber, olives, cherry tomatoes — anything you like!

NEGRONI

Glass: Old fashioned
Garnish: Twist of orange peel and an oversized ice cube

20 ml (⅔ fl oz) Campari
20 ml (⅔ fl oz) sweet vermouth
20 ml (⅔ fl oz) gin

- Pour ingredients into mixing glass and stir until chilled. Strain over oversized ice cube.

- Squeeze orange peel over glass to release the oils before dropping it in.

MOJITO

Glass: Collins glass
Garnish: with sprigs of mint placed vertically in drink and serve.

60ml (2 fl oz) Light Rum
30ml (1 fl oz) Fresh Lime Juice
½ teaspoon Sugar Syrup
60ml (2 fl oz) Soda Water
6 Sprigs of Fresh Mint

- Pour sugar into a chilled collins glass and add 2-3 sprigs of mint. Muddle well and add juice.

- Add crushed ice to half fill glass and stir. Add Rum and stir. Add more crushed ice and soda then stir gently.

- Garnish with sprigs of mint placed vertically in drink and serve.

COSMOPOLITAN

Glass: Martini
Garnish: Orange twist

45 ml (1 ½ fl oz) Absolut Citron
20 ml (⅓ fl oz) triple sec
20 ml (⅔ fl oz) cranberry juice
juice of ½ fresh Lime

- Pour ingredients into a cocktail shaker over ice and shake.

- Strain into chilled glass.

MANHATTAN

Glass: Martini
Garnish: A red cherry in glass or on a toothpick laying on top of the glass

60 ml (2 fl oz) rye whiskey
30 ml (1 fl oz) sweet vermouth
Dash Angostura bitters

• Stir over ice until chilled. Strain into a chilled glass.

Variations:

Dry Manhattan: replace sweet vermouth with dry vermouthand add a twist of lemon.

Perfect Manhattan: replace half the sweet vermouth with dry vermouth.

TOM COLLINS

Glass: Highball
Garnish: serve with a slice of lemon and cherry

30 ml (2 fl oz) lemon juice
60 ml (2 fl oz) gin
15 ml (½ fl oz) sugar syrup
soda water

- Put cracked ice, lemon juice, and gin in a glass.

- Fill with soda water and stir.

MOSCOW MULE

Glass: Copper mug or glass
Garnish: Slice of lime and mint

30 ml (1 fl oz) vodka
½ a lime
ginger beer to top

- Build over ice.

LONG ISLAND ICED TEA

Glass: Highball or hurricane
Garnish: Lemon slices or lemon twist and mint leaves. Serve with straws.

30 ml (1 fl oz) vodka
30 ml (1 fl oz) white rum
30 ml (1 fl oz) Cointreau
30 ml (1 fl oz) tequila
30 ml (1 fl oz) gin
30 ml (1 fl oz) lemon juice
dash of cola
30 ml (1 fl oz) sugar syrup

- Pour all ingredients except for cola into a cocktail shaker over ice and shake. Strain over fresh ice and top with cola.

- The tea-coloured cola is splashed into the cocktail making it slightly unsuitable for a "tea party".

BLACK RUSSIAN

Glass: Old fashioned
Garnish: None
30 ml (1 fl oz) vodka
30 ml (1 fl oz) Kahlúa

- Build over ice.

Many people add cola to this drink and serve it in a highball glass.

Variation:

Black Pearl: replace the Kahlúa with Tia Maria or dark crème de cacao.

HARVEY WALLBANGER

Glass: Highball
Garnish: Orange slice and cherry

45 ml (1 ½ fl oz) vodka
125 ml (4 fl oz) orange juice
15 ml (½ fl oz) vanilla Galliano

- Add vodka and orange juice to glass full of ice and stir. Float Galliano on top of mix and serve.

Hawaiian bartenders will tell you a visiting Irishman called Harvey pin-balled down the corridor to hotel room after a night out. Hence, he was known as "Harvey Wallbanger".

SCREWDRIVER

Glass: Old fashioned
Garnish: Orange wedge or spiral.

45 ml (1½ fl oz) vodka
45 ml (1½ fl oz) orange juice

- Build over ice.

Variations:

A Comfortable Screw: made with 30 ml (1 fl oz)
vodka, 15 ml (1/2 fl oz) Southern Comfort and
topped with orange juice.

A Slow Comfortable Screw: made with the
addition of 15 ml (1/2 fl oz) sloe gin.

A Long Slow Comfortable Screw: a longer drink
served in a highball glass and topped with orange
juice.

**A Long Slow Comfortable Screw Up Against A
Wall**: add of 15 ml (1/2 fl oz) Galliano floated on top
of the drink.

GIMLET

Glass: Old fashioned or coupe
Garnish: Lime wheel

60 ml (2 fl oz) gin
30 ml (1 fl oz) lime juice
15 ml (½ fl oz) sugar syrup

* Pour ingredients into a cocktail shaker. Shake over ice and pour, then add cubed ice.

This cocktail can also be made using pear juice. Adjust sugar syrup to taste

GRASSHOPPER

Glass: Martini or coupe
Garnish: Shaved chocolate and cream

30 ml (1 fl oz) crème de menthe
30 ml (1 fl oz) white crème de cacao
30 ml (1 fl oz) cream

- Pour ingredients into a cocktail shaker over ice and shake.

- Double strain into chilled glass.

Some people prefer dark crème de cacao instead of white crème de cacao.

HURRICANE

Glass: Hurricane glass
Garnish: Orange slice and cherry

30 ml (1 fl oz) Bacardi
30 ml (1 fl oz) orange juice
15 ml (½ fl oz) lime cordial
45 ml (1½ fl oz) lemon juice
45 ml (1½ fl oz) sugar syrup
15 ml Bacardi Gold, to top

- Pour all ingredients except for Bacardi Gold into a cocktail shaker over ice and shake.

- Strain over fresh ice and gently float Bacardi Gold on top.

JAPANESE SLIPPER

Glass: Martini
Garnish: Slice of lemon on side of glass

30 ml (1 fl oz) melon liqueur
30 ml (1 fl oz) Cointreau
30 ml (1 fl oz) lemon juice

- Pour ingredients into a cocktail shaker over ice and shake.

- Strain into chilled glass.

KAMIKAZE

Glass: Martini
Garnish: Lime wheel

30 ml (1 fl oz) vodka
30 ml (1 fl oz) Cointreau
30 ml (1 fl oz) fresh lemon juice
1 teaspoon lime cordial

- Pour ingredients into a cocktail shaker over ice and shake.

- Strain into chilled glass.

MINT JULEP

Glass: Old fashioned
Garnish: Mint

60 ml (2 fl oz) bourbon
10 ml (⅓ fl oz) sugar syrup
2–3 dashes cold water or soda water
8 sprigs of fresh mint
crushed or shaved ice

- Muddle sugar syrup and 5 mint sprigs in a glass until the mint becomes fragrant, but stop before it breaks up.

- Pour into thoroughly frosted glass and pack with ice. Add bourbon and water/soda and mix (with a chopping motion using a long-handled bar spoon).

- Garnish with remaining mint and serve with a straw.

OLD FASHIONED

Glass: Old fashioned
Garnish: Twist of orange peel, cherry, and an oversized icecube

60 ml (2 fl oz) bourbon or rye whiskey
2 dashes bitters
sugar cube

- Place sugar cube in glass, coat with bitters and muddle. Add whiskey and stir until sugar is completely dissolved.

- Add oversized ice cube and squeeze orange peel over the glass to release the oils before dropping in the drink.

Variations:

Rum Old Fashioned: replace bourbon/rye with 60 ml (2 fl oz) brown rum.

CLASSIC DAIQUIRI

Glass: Martini or coupe
Garnish: Lime wheel

45 ml (1½ fl oz) Bacardi
5 ml (⅙ fl oz) grenadine
15 ml (½ fl oz) fresh lime juice

- Pour ingredients into a cocktail shaker over ice and shake.

- Strain into a chilled cocktail glass and serve.

STRAWBERRY DAIQUIRI

Glass: Martini
Garnish: Strawberry

30 ml (1 fl oz) Bacardi
15 ml (½ fl oz) Cointreau
15 ml (½ fl oz) strawberry liqueur
30 ml (1 fl oz) fresh lemon juice
4 fresh strawberries (diced)
fresh strawberry

- Pour Bacardi, Cointreau, liqueur and juice into a blender over small amount of crushed ice then add diced strawberries.

- Blend until smooth and pour into a chilled cocktail glass.

CHOCOLATE MARTINI

Glass: Martini
Garnish: Cocao or chocolate
60 ml (2 fl oz) vodka
15 ml (½ fl oz) white crème de cacao

- Pour ingredients into a cocktail shaker over ice and shake.

- Prepare a cocktail glass with a cocoa powder frosted rim –moistened with cacao.

- Strain into a chilled martini glass and serve.

This drink is also known as Chocolate Monk.

CHOCOLATE MINT MARTINI

Glass: Martini
60 ml (2 fl oz) vodka
30 ml (1 fl oz) white crème de cacao
30 ml (1 fl oz) white crème de menthe

- Prepare a cocktail glass with a cocoa powder frosted rim –moistened with cacao. Pour ingredients into a cocktail shaker over ice and shake. Strain into prepared glass and serve.

FROZEN BANANA DAIQUIRI

Glass: Hurricane or martini glass
Garnish: Banana slice

45 ml (1½ fl oz) Bacardi
15 ml (½ fl oz) fresh lime juice
1 teaspoon sugar syrup
½ fresh banana (diced)
slice of fresh banana

- Pour Bacardi, juice and sugar into a blender over a large amount of crushed ice then add diced

- banana.

- Blend until slushy and pour into a frosted cocktail glass.

- Garnish with a slice of banana then serve.

WATERMELON MARTINI

Glass: Martini
Garnish: A wedge of watermelon

60 ml (2 fl oz) vodka
dash sugar syrup
slice of fresh watermelon (crushed)
wedge of fresh watermelon

- Pour vodka and sugar into a cocktail shaker over ice then add crushed watermelon.

- Shake well and strain into a chilled martini glass.

STRAWBERRY MARGARITA

Glass: Margarita glass

45 ml (1½ fl oz) white tequila
15 ml (½ fl oz) Cointreau
8 ml (¼ fl oz) strawberry liqueur
15 ml (½ fl oz) fresh lemon juice
4 fresh strawberries (diced)
fresh strawberry

- Prepare a margarita glass with a sugar-frosted rim.

- Pour tequila, Cointreau, liqueur and juice into a blender over a large amount of crushed ice then add diced strawberries.

- Blend until slushy and pour into prepared glass. Garnish with a strawberry and serve with a short straw.

VODKA MARTINI

Glass: Martini
Garnish: Lemon twist

60 ml (2 fl oz) vodka
15 ml (½ fl oz) dry vermouth

- Pour vodka and vermouth into a mixing glass over ice then stir until liquid is chilled.

- Strain into a chilled martini glass and garnish with a twist of lemon peel then serve.

GILROY

Glass: Martini or Old Fashion
Garnish : Cherry or Orange peel

30ml (1 fl oz) Gin
30ml (1 fl oz) Cherry Brandy
15ml (½ fl oz) Dry Vermouth
Dash Angostura Bitters
15ml (½ fl oz) Fresh Lemon Juice
Maraschino Cherry
Twist of Orange Peel

- Pour Gin, Brandy, Vermouth, Bitters and juice into a cocktail shaker over ice.

- Shake and strain into a chilled cocktail glass.

- Garnish with a cherry and orange peel then serve.

CORKSCREW

Glass: Old Fashion glass

45ml (1½ fl oz) Light Rum
15ml (½ fl oz) Dry Vermouth
15ml (½ fl oz) Peach Brandy
Spiral of Lemon Peel

- Pour Rum, Vermouth and Brandy into a cocktail shaker over ice.

- Shake and strain into an old-fashioned glass over cracked ice.

- Add lemon peel and serve.

GREYHOUND

Glass: Highball glass

45ml (1½ fl oz) Dry Gin
150ml (5 fl oz) Grapefruit Juice

- Pour Gin into a highball glass over ice and add juice, stir then serve.

WHISKY SOUR

Glass: Old fashioned
Garnish: Red cherry and slice of lemon

60 ml (1 ½ fl oz) Scotch whisky
30 ml (1 fl oz) lemon juice
15 ml (½ fl oz) sugar syrup
½ egg white

- Add ingredients to shaker and shake vigorously for 10-15 seconds without ice.

- Add ice to shaker and shake. Double strain over fresh ice.

Variation:

Amaretto Sour: replace the whisky with Amaretto.

PINEAPPLE DAIQUIRI

Glass: Glass: Hurricane or Martini glass
Garnish: Slice of Pineapple

60ml (2 fl oz) Bacardi
15ml (½ fl oz) Cointreau
15ml (½ fl oz) Fresh Lemon Juice
15ml (½ fl oz) Fresh Lime Juice
6 Pieces of Pineapple (diced)
Slice of Pineapple

- Pour Bacardi, Cointreau and juices into a blender over crushed ice then add diced pineapple.

- Blend and pour into a chilled champagne saucer.

- Garnish with a slice of pineapple and serve.

SANGRIA

Glass: Jug or punch bowl
Garnish: Orange

1 bottle red wine
2 fl oz (60 ml) brandy
2 fl oz (60 ml) white rum
2 fl oz (60 ml) Cointreau
4 cups (1¾ pints/1 litre)
orange juice
2 tsp (10 ml) sugar
selection of chopped fruit
4 cups of ice cubes

- Pour all ingredients into punch bowl with 4 cups ice cubes and stir well. Serve in cocktail glasses.

CAMPARI & SODA

Glass: Old Fashioned
Garnish: Orange Slice

2 fl oz (60 ml) Campari
2 fl oz (60 ml) soda water
1 slice of orange

- Build over ice and stir well.

- Garnish with slice of orange.

WHITE RUSSIAN

Glass: Old Fashioned
Garnish: None

2 fl oz (60 ml) vodka
1 fl oz (30 ml) white crème de cacao
1 fl oz (30 ml) double (heavy) cream

- Shake all ingredients with ice in a shaker and strain into glass.

BRANDY ALEXANDER

Glass: Martini or Coupe
Garnish: None

1 fl oz (30 ml) brandy
1 fl oz (30 ml) dark crème de cacao
1 fl oz (30 ml) double (heavy) cream
ground nutmeg
1 cherry

- Shake all ingredients except nutmeg and
- cherry with ice in a shaker and strain into glass.
- Garnish with nutmeg, then skewer cherry with a cocktail stick and add to glass.

GODFATHER

Glass: Old Fashioned
Garnish: Orange Wheel

1 fl oz (30 ml) Scotch whisky
1 fl oz (30 ml) Amaretto

- Mix together and then pour into glass over ice and stir.

AMERICANO

Glass: Old fashioned
Garnish: Orange wedge

30 ml (1 fl oz) Campari
30 ml (1 fl oz) rosso vermouth
soda water, to top

- Build over ice and top up with soda water.

- Originated from European travellers visiting

- America desiring a taste of European aperitifs.

BELLINI

Glass: Champagne flute
Garnish: None

45 ml (1 ½ fl oz) peach purée
sparkling wine, to top

* Pour puree into glass and add sparkling, stirring gently.

This drink is traditionally made using white peaches.

SALTY DOG

Glass: Old Fashioned
Garnish: Grapefruit slice

45 ml (1 ½ fl oz) vodka
grapefruit juice, to top

- Build over ice.

Straws are generally unnecessary, drink the cocktail from the salt rim.

SEX ON THE BEACH

Glass: Hurricane
Garnish: Orange slice and cherry

30 ml (1 fl oz) vodka
30 ml (1 fl oz) peach schnapps
60 ml (2 fl oz) cranberry juice
60 ml (2 fl oz) orange juice.

- Build over ice.

- Adding the cranberry juice last will give the drink a beautiful swirling effect

TEQUILA SUNRISE

Glass: Highball
Garnish: Orange wheel, a red cherry.

30 ml tequila
1 teaspoon grenadine
orange juice, to top

- Build over ice.

To obtain the cleanest visual effect, drop grenadine down the inside of the glass, after topping up with orange juice.

Dropping grenadine in the middle creates a fallout effect, detracting from the presentation of the cocktail. Best served with chilled, freshly squeezed orange juice.

Variation:

Vodka Sunrise: replace tequila with vodka.

SIDECAR

Glass: Martini
Garnish: Lemon or organge twist optional

30 ml (1 fl oz) brandy
20 ml Cointreau*
20 ml lemon juice

- Pour ingredients into a cocktail shaker over ice and shake.

- Strain into chilled glass. Salted or unsalted rim optional.

Cointreau may be substituted with triple sec.

INDEX

Classic Cocktails

First published in 2022 by New Holland Publishers, Sydney

Level 1, 178 Fox Valley Road, Wahroonga, 2076, NSW, Australia

newhollandpublishers.com

A record of this book is held at the National Library of Australia

ISBN : 9781760795559

Group Managing Director: Fiona Schultz
Designer: Ben Taylor (Taylor Design)
Project Editor: Elise James
Production Director: Arlene Gippert
Printed in China

10 9 8 7 6 5 4 3 2 1

Keep up with New Holland Publishers

 NewHollandPublishers

 @newhollandpublishers